This Notebook
Belongs To

_____

_____

Date:

To-Do List

Appointments

Date:

To-Do List

Appointments

Date:

To-Do List

Appointments

Date:

To-Do List

Appointments

Date:

To-Do List

Appointments

Date:

To-Do List

Appointments

Date:

To-Do List

Appointments

Date:

To-Do List

Appointments

Date:

To-Do List

Appointments

Date:

To-Do List

Appointments

Date:

To-Do List

Appointments

Date:

To-Do List

Appointments

Date:

To-Do List

Appointments

Date:

To-Do List

Appointments

Date:

To-Do List

Appointments

Date:

To-Do List

Appointments

Date:

To-Do List

Appointments

Date:

To-Do List

Appointments

Date:

To-Do List

Appointments

Date:

To-Do List

Appointments

Date:

To-Do List

Appointments

Date:

To-Do List

Appointments

Date:

To-Do List

Appointments

Date:

To-Do List

Appointments

Date:

To-Do List

Appointments

Date:

To-Do List

Appointments

Date:

To-Do List

Appointments

Date:

To-Do List

Appointments

Date:

To-Do List

Appointments

Date:

To-Do List

Appointments

Date:

To-Do List

Appointments

Date:

To-Do List

Appointments

Date:

To-Do List

Appointments

Date:

To-Do List

Appointments

Date:

To-Do List

Appointments

Date:

To-Do List

Appointments

Date:

To-Do List

Appointments

Date:

To-Do List

Appointments

Date:

To-Do List

Appointments

Date:

To-Do List

Appointments

Date:

To-Do List

Appointments

Date:

To-Do List

Appointments

Date:

To-Do List

Appointments

Date:

To-Do List

Appointments

Date:

To-Do List

Appointments

Date:

To-Do List

Appointments

Date:

To-Do List

Appointments

Date:

To-Do List

Appointments

Date:

To-Do List

Appointments

Date:

To-Do List

Appointments

Date:

To-Do List

Appointments

Date:

To-Do List

Appointments

Date:

To-Do List

Appointments

Date:

To-Do List

Appointments

Date:

To-Do List

Appointments

Date:

To-Do List

Appointments

Date:

To-Do List

Appointments

Date:

To-Do List

Appointments

Date:

To-Do List

Appointments

Date:

To-Do List

Appointments

Date:

To-Do List

Appointments

Date:

To-Do List

Appointments

Date:

To-Do List

Appointments

Date:

To-Do List

Appointments

Date:

To-Do List

Appointments

Date:

To-Do List

Appointments

Date:

To-Do List

Appointments

Date:

To-Do List

Appointments

Date:

To-Do List

Appointments

Date:

To-Do List

Appointments

Date:

To-Do List

Appointments

Date:

To-Do List

Appointments

Date:

To-Do List

Appointments

Date:

To-Do List

Appointments

Date:

To-Do List

Appointments

Date:

To-Do List

Appointments

Date:

_____
_____
_____
_____
_____
_____
_____
_____
_____
_____
_____
_____
_____
_____
_____
_____
_____
_____
_____

To-Do List

Appointments

Date:

To-Do List

Appointments

Date:

To-Do List

Appointments

Date:

To-Do List

Appointments

Date:

To-Do List

Appointments

Date:

To-Do List

Appointments

Date:

To-Do List

Appointments

Date:

To-Do List

Appointments

Date:

To-Do List

Appointments

Date:

To-Do List

Appointments

Date:

To-Do List

Appointments

Date:

To-Do List

Appointments

Date:

To-Do List

Appointments

Date:

To-Do List

Appointments

Date:

To-Do List

Appointments

Date:

To-Do List

Appointments

Date:

To-Do List

Appointments

Date:

To-Do List

Appointments

Date:

To-Do List

Appointments

Date:

To-Do List

Appointments

Date:

To-Do List

Appointments

Date:

To-Do List

Appointments

Date:

To-Do List

Appointments

Date:

To-Do List

Appointments

Date:

To-Do List

Appointments

Date:

To-Do List

Appointments

Date:

To-Do List

Appointments

Date:

To-Do List

Appointments

Date:

To-Do List

Appointments

Date:

To-Do List

Appointments

Date:

To-Do List

Appointments

Date:

To-Do List

Appointments

Date:

To-Do List

Appointments

Date:

To-Do List

Appointments

Date:

To-Do List

Appointments

Date:

To-Do List

Appointments

Date:

To-Do List

Appointments

Date:

To-Do List

Appointments

Date:

To-Do List

Appointments

Date:

To-Do List

Appointments

Date:

To-Do List

Appointments

Date:

To-Do List

Appointments

Date:

To-Do List

Appointments

Made in the USA
Las Vegas, NV
20 May 2022